MAKING
SAMPLERS

New & Traditional Designs

Jutta Lammer

Sterling Publishing Co. Inc. New York

Distributed in the U.K. by Blandford Press

Library of Congress Cataloging in Publication Data

Lammèr, Jutta.
  Making samplers.

  Translation of: Alte und neue Stickmustertücher zum
Nacharbeiten.
  Bibliography: p.
  Includes index.
  1. Samplers. 2. Cross-stitch—Patterns. 3. Embroidery
—Patterns. I. Title.
TT775.L3313 1984   746.3   83-24240
ISBN 0-8069-5510-4
ISBN 0-8069-7772-8 (pbk.)

Translated by Hannah Meyer

Contents

EVENWEAVE COMPUTATION CHART

NUMBER OF STITCHES IN DESIGN (HEIGHT OR WIDTH)

STITCHES PER INCH IN FABRIC

	20	30	40	50	55	60	65	70	75	80	85	90	95	100	105	110	115	120	125	130	135	140	145	150	155	160	165	170	180	190	200	210	220	230	240	250
11	1⅞	2¾	3⅝	4½	5	5½	5⅞	6⅜	6⅞	7¼	7¾	8¼	8⅝	9⅛	9½	10	10½	10⅞	11⅜	11⅞	12¼	12¾	13¼	13⅝	14¼	14½	15	15½	16⅜	17¼	18¼	19⅛	20	21	21⅞	22¾
13	1½	2⅜	3	3⅞	4¼	4⅝	5	5⅜	5½	6⅛	6½	6⅞	7⅜	7⅝	8	8½	8⅞	9¼	9⅝	10	10⅜	10¾	11⅛	11½	11⅞	12⅜	12⅝	13⅛	13⅞	14⅝	15⅜	16⅛	17	17⅝	18½	19¼
14	1⅜	2⅛	2⅞	3½	3⅞	4¼	4⅝	5	5⅜	5¾	6	6⅜	6¾	7⅛	7½	7⅞	8¼	8½	8⅞	9¼	9⅝	10	10⅜	10¾	11⅛	11½	11¾	12⅛	12⅞	13½	14¼	15	15¾	16⅜	17⅛	17⅞
18	1⅛	1⅝	2¼	2¾	3	3⅜	3⅝	3⅞	4¼	4½	4¾	5	5¼	5½	5⅞	6⅛	6⅜	6⅝	7	7¼	7½	7¾	8	8⅜	8⅝	8⅞	9	9⅜	10	10½	11⅛	11⅝	12¼	12¾	13	13⅞
22	⅞	1⅜	1⅞	2¼	2½	2¾	3	3⅛	3⅜	3⅝	3⅞	4⅛	4⅜	4½	4¾	5	5¼	5½	5⅝	5⅞	6⅛	6⅜	6½	6⅞	7	7¼	7½	7¾	8⅛	8⅝	9⅛	9½	10	10½	11	11⅜
25	¾	1⅛	1½	2	2¼	2⅜	2⅝	2⅞	3	3¼	3⅜	3⅝	3⅞	4	4¼	4⅜	4⅝	4⅞	5	5¼	5⅜	5⅝	5⅞	6	6¼	6½	6⅝	6⅞	7¼	7⅝	8	8⅜	8⅞	9¼	9⅝	10
26	¾	1⅛	1½	1⅞	2⅛	2¼	2½	2¾	2⅞	3⅛	3¼	3½	3⅝	3⅞	4	4¼	4⅜	4⅝	4¾	5	5¼	5⅜	5½	5¾	6	6⅛	6⅜	6½	7	7⅜	7⅝	8	8½	8⅞	9¼	9⅝

WASHING INSTRUCTIONS FOR COUNTED CROSS STITCH
1. A brief soak in cold water (5 minutes or less).
2. Wash in lukewarm water using ½ to 1 tsp. of Ivory Snow powder.
3. Rinse well in cool water.
4. Soak briefly (again, 5 minutes or less) in a weak solution of 1 tsp. white vinegar (1 tsp. salt may be substituted) to 1 quart of cool water
5. Rinse well. "Squeeze" excess water from stitchery but **never** "wring."
6. Roll in a clean towel for a brief time.
7. While still wet, iron embroidery on **wrong** side on a double thickness of towels. Iron with the grain of fabric so as not to pull out of shape.
8. Place ironed stitchery on a towel and allow to air dry 24 hours before framing.

Reproduced with permission of The Sewing Bird (4014 Chicago Drive, Grandville, MI 48418)

Historical Development

The origin of the embroidery sampler is unknown, but there is evidence from Asia that it has existed since the ninth century. On a fourteenth century wall hanging in the Church of San Francisco in Barcelona, women are portrayed embroidering—possibly engaged in the making of samplers. The oldest sampler of English origin dates from 1598 and is on exhibit in the Victoria and Albert Museum in London. This sampler, which was not discovered until 1960, has the following details:

Row 1: Stylized tree with perched bird (owl?) in the center; dog with a curved tail and a collar; stylized tree with squirrel on the left branch and a bird's nest with three fledglings in the center; carnation bouquet with three blossoms next to the letters IVNO (Juno?), next to a little dog.

Row 2: A small griffin, a bear, over a border of leaves; a reclining deer (as portrayed in *Schönsperger's Pattern Book* of 1597).[1]

A detail of an English sampler from 1830 illustrating various large and small letters and small border rows. The smallest letters in block form are hardly larger than a pinhead. Black wool yarn on natural colored linen, 16″ × 13″ (41 × 33 cm). The mystery of the missing letters, especially the J, in many regional samplers dates back to the early times when the alphabet included 24 letters. German and Dutch samplers, particularly, reflect the Latin influence on the alphabet since the early alphabet did not include a J, V or W and the U was shaped like a V. Throughout this book, these variations recur in old samplers and, interestingly, were perpetuated in many contemporary samplers. Private collection.

Small sampler, probably a school work, which was finished the 28th of January, 1870. Each letter had to be embroidered twice for practice. Colorful wool yarn on an edged cotton fabric, 11¾" × 8" (30 × 20 cm). Private collection.

Row 3: Alphabet in capital letters and the name JANE BOSOCKE with the numbers 1598.

Rows 4 and 5: ALICE LEE WAS BORN IN THE NOVEMBER BEING TUESDAY IN THE AFTERNOONE 1596.

The remainder of the sampler is decorated with vines, fruits and blossoms, as well as with geometric motifs.

Presumably this sampler was created in commemmoration of the birth of the child Alice Lee and only dated for this reason. The Scandinavian countries are especially known for such commemorative samplers from the nineteenth century and later.

**Sampler from Brazil, 1885, worked by a convent scholar. Red cotton thread (faded) on handwoven linen with hem-stitched edges.
Engel Textile Museum, Hamburg.**

Written accounts indicate, nevertheless, that samplers existed in Europe at an earlier time. For example, in the household account book of 1502 of the English royal house there is an order for the delivery of a yard of linen to make a sampler for Queen Elizabeth of York: "For a sampler for the Queen."

Samplers appear in various languages explaining the use and purposes of this handwork: Samplers served as patterns for future handwork; they were used as identification labels for clothing. Nevertheless, one cannot overlook the high artistic value of the embroideries produced. In addition, two aspects are significant: There are valuable silk embroideries produced in great numbers by the high-ranking ladies of society, of fine patterns and designs in indescribable embroidery variations, embroideries were also produced as an art form in a social setting.

Sampler from 1736, believed to be the design of a specially commissioned artist. Stitches include petit point, gros point, Florentine stitch, stem stitch, satin stitch, cross stitch, and French knots. Silk thread on linen fabric.
Museum for Arts and Crafts, Hamburg.
(Photo: Bauer-Hamersen)

Young girls practiced the art of needlework and hung their successfully completed results, framed behind glass, in their parents' home. Exhibited on highly visible walls, the handwork impressed prospective suitors with the girls' artistic ability, patience, and diligence. Originally, samplers served both as home decoration and to identify the family. Since 1523, there have been printed pattern samplers.

They were, generally, too expensive for the average person.

For centuries, children, especially young girls, were instructed in needlework by grandmothers and mothers, and in affluent families by nuns and specialized embroidery teachers. It was not until 1872, in Prussia, that needlework instruction in the general schools and institutions of learning was introduced.

American sampler by Mary Emily James, aged 11, 1867. Early samplers were found in Massachusetts in 1630; on Long Island, 1713; in New Hampshire, 1719; in New York, 1720; in Connecticut, 1721; in Pennsylvania, 1724; in Rhode Island, 1725; in Vermont, 1728; in Southern California, 1734; in New Jersey, 1740; in Delaware, 1747; in Maine, 1750; in Georgia, 1763; in Virginia, 1765; in Maryland, 1766; in North Carolina, 1786; in Kentucky, 1800; and in Ohio, 1807.

Sampler from 1880. Letters, worked in satin and stem stitch, were embroidered in schools as part of the lessons in needlework. Cotton thread in Turkish red on linen. Engel Textile Museum, Hamburg.

Girls learned embroidery along with knitting, mending and darning. Many planned samplers, consisting of various letters and numerals, as well as different borders and ornaments. Numerous early samplers from school instruction have survived intact. They predominate in cross stitch worked in Turkish red on linen or cotton fabric. From 1872 until the end of World War I, needlework courses were required.

Later, another kind of sampler—also red on white—was finished in straight stitch and contained alphabets, numerals and various all-white embroideries. Some samplers were embroidered in three colors: white with red and blue; less frequently, white with red and yellow. The background of the latter was linen or cotton firm even weave, which was purchased already stamped.

In 1881, Emmy Rossel, director of a girls' high school in Berlin, published a *Guide for the Instruction of Women's Needlework*,[2] including a complete copy of a sampler in satin stitch. In 1889, Julie Legorju of Kassel wrote *Needlework Instruction as Class Instruction*,[3] which included instructions for samplers in counted cross stitch

French sampler embroidered in
Paris in 1919, presumably student
work. Red cotton thread on loosely
woven cotton, edged with machine-
made lace.
Engel Textile Museum, Hamburg.

technique. These classic works perpetuated for many decades production of the same samplers, thus suppressing the girls' creativity. Through this repetition, however, the technique was perfected. After World War I, needlework instruction changed to focus only on useful items. Patterns were still embroidered in rows on cloth, however. The finished embroideries were generally used for bags, pillowcases, and other uses.

This lovely art endured for many generations as a pleasurable hobby among mature women. Since the 1960s samplers regained importance and currently have become collectors' items— antiques.

One of the most beautiful privately owned collections in Europe is to be found in Buxtehude, in Lower Saxony. Elfi and Hans-Joachim Connemann collected three hundred rare pieces within a decade. The most expensive piece was valued at approximately $3,000 during the 53rd auction of the *Hauses Waltraud Boltz* in Bayreuth, in September, 1981. It was sold for approximately $2,400. This magnificent multi-colored sampler dates from

1748, is 14¼″ × 15¼″ (36 × 39 cm), worked with silk on the finest linen. Another sampler, declared to be from the seventeenth to eighteenth century, although undated, was sold for approximately $1,500. Embroidered with silk thread on silk fabric, this sampler also features appliqué work and measures 23″ × 25½″ (58 × 65 cm). The buyers are not museums, as one might assume, but rather, are private collectors with limited financial resources who wished to preserve these relics of a past embroidery culture.

Designing
and Reproducing
Samplers

Secular and religious motifs are found together on many samplers. All of the motifs and symbols cannot be identified. For example, the newly designed sampler on page 81 illustrates the best-known designs of the traditional collected treasures.

Bible illustrations and church paintings were used as patterns for religious subjects by talented embroiderers, often pastors' wives. Secular motifs were often copied from valuable textiles imported to Europe from the Far East. In addition, affluent women commissioned artists to design exclusive embroideries. Magnificent nature and hunting scenes were created in this manner (see page 8, a sampler embroidered in silk).

At the beginning of the sixteenth century, commercially printed designs became available. These designs also could have been used for weaving, lacemaking, and filet work and were called "sample books." They included designs of the publisher and also well-known designs. Many of the latter originated in the Far East on fine textiles.

The first sample book appeared in 1523 in Augsburg under the title, *Model or Design Booklet*,[4] from the publisher Schönsperger. It included twenty-four woodcuts. Schönsperger later published the title, *A New Pattern Book*. The pattern drawings were usually supplied with a grid or graph.

In 1529, a pattern book by Peter Quentel appeared with a wood carver, an embroiderer, a (lacemaker?) needleworker, and a weaver illustrated on the title page. The

Very interesting sampler, circa 1920. Here, various stitches and their variations, rather than patterns of design, are represented. It was probably an instruction sampler for embroidery lessons. Techniques with numerous textures: satin stitch, chain stitch, cross stitch, Florentine stitch. Cotton twist (formerly called *glanzgarn*) on linen evenweave. Engel Textile Museum, Hamburg.

French cross stitch pattern, colored by hand, from 1850. The motifs were provided with a color key, as in the counted patterns; for each color there was a different symbol on the drawing. The background was filled in with a solid color.

title, *A New Pattern Book for All Artists,*[6] included the subtitle, *For Use of the Woodcarver, Embroiderers of Coats-of-Arms, Specialty Embroiderers, and Others.* Printed in Old German, and published in Cologne, this book was reprinted in 1529 in Leipzig.

In 1597 in Nürnberg, Johann Sibmacher's *Beautiful New Pattern Book*[7] appeared which—like Schönsperger's—contained numerous counted patterns available on graphed charts. This book, with many editions, became the best-liked

pattern thesaurus of the embroiderers, especially in South Germany. Sibmacher's subjects, especially a peacock and a reclining deer, can be seen until the late nineteenth century in many remaining samplers and handwork. The last known edition of this book was printed in 1877.

Sibmacher's pattern book, interestingly, illustrated the same designs found in its predecessor published in Strassburg in 1589—a pattern book by B. Jobin. B. Jobin's book contained primarily animal illustrations. It

13

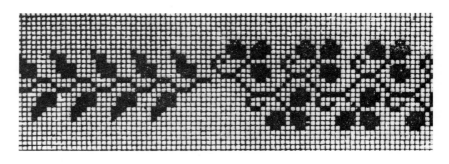

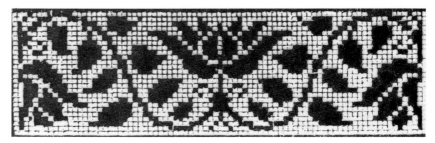

is not certain, however, whether this book was planned as an inspiration for embroideries. In 1676 a pattern book came out in Nürnberg by Rosina Fürst, who, in contrast to her predecessor, presented her own designs and illustrated patterns.

In 1795, *A Drawing, Painting and Embroidery Book for Self-Instruction for Ladies*[8] was published in Leipzig by artist Johann Friedrich Netto. Each copy included a completely embroidered sampler in finest work and 48 hand-colored engravings. The pattern choices demonstrated that this book was intended only for an exclusive clientele.

Subsequently, new methods included transfer patterns which were drawn on tissue paper, copper stencils (for smaller embroideries and monograms), and stamped patterns on printed fabrics. For example, E. Rossel, successor to the firm A. Massengier in Potsdam, used these transfer patterns at the beginning of the twentieth century.

Fibres and Embroidery Techniques

Cross stitch patterns were embroidered on linen and wool fabrics and later on canvas. These textiles were woven of equally spaced vertical (warp) and horizontal (filling or weft) threads, thereby producing a uniform background or evenweave. For other embroidery techniques such as free style—not counted types—silk, the finest wool, linen and later, cotton fibres were used. The threads or yarns for cross stitch works were of linen and wool, less frequently silk, and for embroideries other than counted types, silk and linen fibres. Until the introduction of aniline dyes in 1860, all yarns were dyed from natural sources.

On various textiles, one finds in addition to the traditional cross stitch, the four-sided stitch, the Holbein or double running stitch, the backstitch and the half cross stitch. One can see on the back of these works, cross stitch, crosses, four-sided and straight stitches, de-pending on the age and ability of the embroiderer.

Embroideries, not counted types, often incorporated many kinds of stitches, particularly the satin stitch or shading stitch. Some scenes appear to have been "painted" with a needle and developed into a style known as needle painting. For monograms, sampler alphabets, and numerals, the satin stitch and its many variations were preferred. Some embroideries were edged with stem stitch, knot stitch, buttonhole and chain stitch variations. These and basket stitch variations are to be found in greatest quantities on old samplers.

Interestingly, samplers in white embroidery were often enriched with lace inserts. As a rule, the old samplers are hemmed on two sides where the embroidery fabric has no selvage. Many samplers are lovingly edged with silk ribbon and trimmed at the corners with rosettes.

Samplers Today

The love of embroidering has never ceased. Girls and women always have dedicated themselves to this beautiful hobby. Samplers from the 1920s prove that the hobby flourished until 1930. About 1928, Gertrude Caspari issued an instruction booklet with patterns for cross stitch designs. This publication sold nearly 400,000 copies, sponsored by the yarn factory of Wolf Brothers in Pleisse, Saxony.

In addition, the thread manufacturer D.M.C. (Dollfuss, Mieg and Company) in Mulhouse, published design books for cross stitch works from which samplers were patterned. But the largest achievement in continuing the sampler tradition in the Scandinavian countries, and in a large part of Germany, undoubtedly has been that of the Danish Handwork Guild, *Haandarbejdets Fremme*, under the Danish queen's patronage. Incentives for preserving and renewing the

Sampler embroidered from the 1929 pattern book, *Vereins der Dresdner Nadelarbeits-Lehrerinnen* by Gertrude Caspari (Association of the Dresden Needlework Teachers). Collection Bahmann, Hannover.

art of needlework, especially embroidery, often came from this Guild. *Haandarbejdets Fremme* has engaged artists of international fame to develop new embroidery patterns, providing new stimulation for traditional ideas.

Embroiderers can still obtain natural-colored linen thread in the finest grades and natural linen backgrounds available throughout the world. A large number of the projects in this book were made with Danish fabrics and threads; it is possible to substitute other fabric and yarns such as cotton, wool or other fibres.

Since the late 1960s, especially, young women as well as men have again become enthusiastic about needlework, including the embroidery of samplers. Handwork publications and women's magazines often supply embroidery patterns. The design collection in this book has not previously been published in the English language.

Techniques

Supplies

To create samplers in this book, you will need supplies such as fabrics, thread or yarn and needles. Suggestions are given in the text along with each specific sampler. Also, for cross stitch work, the evenweave fabric is identified by threads per inch, usually fine, medium or coarser weaves. The general rule: The smaller the number, the larger the weave; the higher the number, the finer the weave.* For example, evenweave with 24 threads per inch will make 12 crosses (a cross is always embroidered over 2 vertical and horizontal threads); evenweave with 21 threads per inch will make 10.5 crosses; evenweave with 14 threads per inch will make 7 crosses.

Evenweave fabrics are available in linen, cotton or mixed fibres. If you plan an embroidery with a coarser fabric than suggested in the project, buy more fabric than the given amount; the motifs will be much larger when worked on a coarser fabric.

Embroidery threads should be matched to the fabric textures by using from one to 5 or 6 strands. After cutting your working thread, separate the strands to lay them flat before threading the needle, whether you use 2 or 6 strands. Always try out a sample on your fabric scrap before deciding how many strands you should use.

When you work on evenweaves and you wish to calculate the height or width of your motif, please refer to the "Evenweave Computation Chart," page 4.

Needles should be short (tapestry or canvas) and must have a dull point for counted embroideries. For linen number 24, use one strand cotton thread and needle number 24; for linen 21 use one strand thread and needle number 22; for linen number 14, use 2 strands and needle number 21. General rule: Finer needles have higher numbers; heavier needles, lower numbers.

For embroideries on very fine fabrics, not counted types, use fine white cotton fabrics such as batiste or fine linens. Embroider with one strand cotton thread or silk, if you wish, and a very sharp needle with eye suitable for thickness of your thread. It may be necessary to use an embroidery frame for very fine work.

Transferring Patterns

For counted embroideries, transferring is easy. Using bright colored cotton sewing thread, baste the vertical and horizontal center lines of your fabric (remove when embroidering is completed). Count from the *center top* the fabric threads to begin the first motif (two threads equal one half cross). The simplest point to begin embroidering is at the top row center (for example, a letter) and then proceed towards the left and right. Through this row you have a good beginning for subsequent counting while following the pattern chart.

Patterns of free style embroideries (not counted types) can be transferred as follows: Draw motifs of your choice on tracing paper; lay transfer paper (available at art and hobby stores in grey, red, yellow, blue and white colors) with color side *down* on the fabric top and spread the tracing paper with your motif over the transfer paper. Using a ball-point pen, trace the pattern through to the fabric. To embroider, cover the tracing line with your thread or yarn choices.

*When using evenweave (linen, cotton or any fibre) and working over 2 threads per stitch, the fabric count is divided in half in order to determine how many stitches per inch.

This illustrates the back of a cross stitch embroidery; vertical and horizontal stitches are formed in back when crosses are formed on the right side. Beginning and ending threads are anchored into stitches of the same color (on the back of the work) and all thread tips are cut off. As a result, the back is very neat and tidy.

Embroidering

When embroidering even-weave fabrics, observe the following principles: Always stitch *between* the fabric threads; never stitch *on* the fabric threads; do not stitch in the embroidery threads; always pull the embroidery thread with even tension so that an equal thread cross is formed in the cross stitch; avoid pulling together the fabric threads (as in pulled thread and open work which form lacy holes in the motifs). And when working with a double thread, work so that the two threads in the embroidery lie parallel to each other, not twisted.

When beginning a new thread, never make a knot. Instead, leave about 2½" (6 cm) hanging loose on the back of the embroidery where you begin. Or, if you have already begun to work, slip the needle into the back stitches to anchor the thread (always into the same color). When you have finished the thread, re-thread the needle (with the loose end) and work it into the stitches of the same color. Cut all ends so that the back of the work is as neat as the front (the sign of a good embroiderer).

Cross stitch may be worked from left to right (as shown in illustration) or beginning from right to left, but be sure that the upper half of all stitches on your embroidery lie in the same direction. Bring needle out at the lower left-hand side of the row, insert the needle 2 threads up and 2 threads to the right and bring needle out 2 threads down to form a half cross. Continue forming parallel diagonal half cross stitches to complete the row and then return to make the complete crosses, working right to left. For large crosses, insert needle 4 threads up and 4 right.

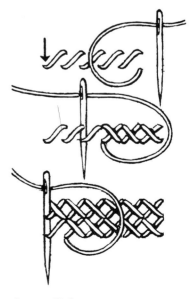

Cross stitch

Other stitches are made as follows: *Satin stitch* follows a drawing outlined with small back stitches. Begin with round forms (leaves, blossoms, dots) in the center of the work in which one stitches. Stitch diagonally from the one contour to the other over the fabric so that it lies smooth and flat (see satin stitch, oblique, illustration). With curved forms, set the inner stitches closer than the outer so as to achieve a fan shape. The contour stitches are tightly embroidered to achieve a sculptured effect. As a rule, satin stitches run diagonally from lower left to upper right, although there are variations (see illustrations on this page).

Florentine stitch is worked in zigzag patterns in 2 or more colors to create a wavy pattern. The size of the wave and the number of threads over which the stitches are worked may be varied. All stitches should be vertical and even lengths.

Florentine stitch

Back stitch is used for outlines and details. Bring the thread out at the right-hand side of the design. Take a stitch backwards the size you need and bring the needle out an equal space from where it first emerged. Continue working right to left, keeping stitches even.

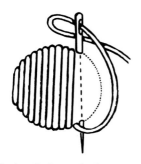

Satin stitch, vertical

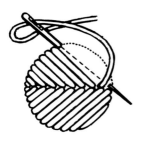

Satin stitch, oblique

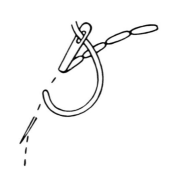

Back stitch

Stem stitch can be worked in an upward or downward direction, or horizontally from left to right (see illustration). After the first stitch from the fabric back to the front, skip several fabric threads, then stitch back to half of the skipped threads and pull the needle through; again skip several fabric threads in the previous length, bring the needle up halfway and continue to embroider. Working with this method, a cord effect to the right is achieved. If you lay the thread down with each needle stitch upward, the cord effect moves to the left.

Stem stitch, moving right

Stem stitch, moving left

French knot is worked as follows: Bring the thread out where the French knot will be placed, hold the thread down with the left thumb, and twist the thread twice or three times around the needle (as shown in illustration). Holding the thread firmly, twist the needle back and insert it close to where thread first emerged. Pull thread through to back and secure (if making only one knot), or bring needle up where next French knot is desired and repeat.

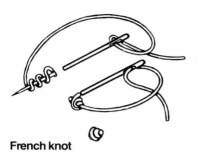

French knot

Buttonhole or *blanket stitch* is embroidered from left to right with the needle pointing in a downward direction. Bring thread out on the lower line, insert the needle in position in the upper line and take a straight downward stitch with the thread under the needle. Pull up the stitch to form a loop and repeat, working close together or farther apart, as the motif requires. Various rows of padding stitches are used as foundations for surfaces or lines of embroidery.

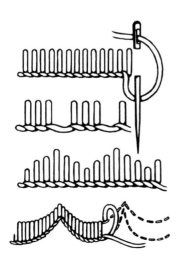

Buttonhole stitch variations

Double running or *Holbein stitch* is worked from right to left. Make a row of running stitches with upper stitches of equal length and under stitches half the size or less of the upper stitches, following the shape of your design. On the return journey, work from left to right, filling in the spaces left in the first journey.

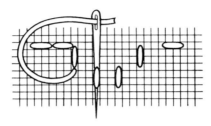

Double running or Holbein stitch

Chain stitch is worked on lines or curves. Bring the thread out at top of the line and hold down with left thumb. Insert needle where it had first emerged, bring point out a short distance away and pull the thread through, keeping the working thread *under* the needle.

Chain stitch

Four-sided stitch can be used as a border or filling. Bring needle up at lower right, insert needle up along the same thread 4 threads higher, angle needle and bring out 4 threads to the left and 4 threads down (see illustration #1); insert needle at original starting point and bring out 4 threads to the left and 4 threads up (illustration #2); insert needle at A and bring out 4 threads down and 4 to the left (illustration #3). Close to make one *four-sided stitch* or continue to end of row. When filling, turn the fabric around for each successive row and pull all stitches firmly.

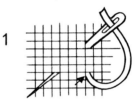

1

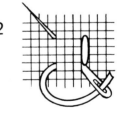

2

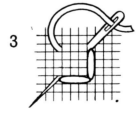

3

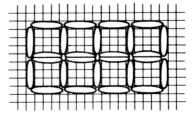

Four-sided stitch

Designing

To personally design and work cross stitch patterns you need graph paper with square grids available at art and stationery stores. If possible, the squares on the graph paper should correspond to the size of the crosses on the planned embroidery; this will help you imagine the height and width of the patterns. If necessary, you can make graph paper using standard square paper and adjusting the size of the squares both vertically and horizontally to fit your pattern, and to fit the size of your fabric's weave.

Using a pencil, draw the desired motif with all details on the graph paper. Then, using ink or a soft-tip marker, cover with a cross all squares through which a line runs. The pencil lines can then be erased. Now correct or complete the form through the changed crosses. Should you desire to color the pattern, paint the motif sections with watercolors, colored markers or colored pencils. Use this chart as a guide when you work your embroidery.

When designing for free style, not counted, embroideries, you may draw the motif on tracing paper and transfer according to the directions on page 18 ("Transferring Patterns"). Or, you may prefer to use a transfer pencil (available at hobby stores). Draw the design on tracing paper with a regular pencil; turn the paper over and using the transfer pencil, draw the entire design on the back. Lay the pattern with the transfer pencil *down* on the fabric to be embroidered. Using a hot iron transfer the design. (The blue lines will disappear after the first washing.) This is a simple method, but care must be taken to be sure all designs are transferred.

If you wish to create an embroidery like the original, proceed as follows: The drawn motif is covered with transparent paper, as described above. With a black soft-tip pen, draw the entire pattern. Then separate the transparent paper from the original; turn over and trace the visible lines with the transfer pencil. Baste the transparent paper with the copied side on the fabric; then the original pattern can be transferred with a hot iron.

The sampler with the alphabet and the butterflies on page 41 was designed and transferred in this way. With the ironing method, it is especially important that the fabric and ironing pattern are well pinned or basted so that nothing can slip. Should a mishap occur, however, you can wash the fabric and use it again.

Finishing

Avoid washing the finished embroidery, if possible, by keeping it immaculately clean while working. To press: lay the work with the right side down on a smooth white cloth; cover it with a white, dampened cloth. Then press with warm iron until the top cloth is dry. With all embroideries, it is important to watch that the work is not pulled during ironing. For this reason, pin it to the right-hand corner of the ironing cloth. If the fabric is so wrinkled that it will not become smooth, dip it into lukewarm water and spread it out to dry flat on a table after smoothing it out to its proper shape. When still damp, lightly iron the embroidery on the wrong side, as suggested above.

Should the embroidery be framed, fold the unseamed edges around a piece of acid-free cardboard slightly smaller in size. With large back and forth stitches across the back, the opposite folds will be stretched evenly.

Designs and Projects

**Samplers
and Embroidery
Patterns**

Embroiderers who have never done cross stitch should best begin with a simple sampler containing small motifs with uncompli- cated changes of color. As you can see on the embroidery detail below, you can work with double strands of cotton embroidery threads.

Wreath and Animal Motif Sampler

Beginners will enjoy working this easy sampler: You will need: *Fabric*: Evenweave 14 threads per inch (see "Techniques," page 18), 21¾" × 16½" (55 × 42 cm) including 1¼" (3 cm) for seam allowance on four sides. The finished piece is 17¾" × 12½" (45 × 32 cm). *Thread*: 2 strands cotton embroidery thread. *Colors*: See chart below corresponding to symbol script on pages 25 and 95. *Needle*: Canvas needle with dull point, number 21.

On the counting pattern, the vertical and horizontal centers are shown at the arrows. Before beginning the embroidering, baste these centers on the fabric using a sewing thread (these will be removed after you complete the work). Begin the embroidery with the letter "F" (top row) and continue working left and right. Now you have a beginning to count the remaining letters, numbers, and motifs. The border is embroidered last.

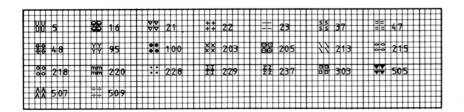

Left
Color symbol chart corresponding to pages 25 and 95. For colors refer to color chart on page 95.
Right
Counting pattern for sampler on page 23 and above.
The arrows indicate the vertical and horizontal centers.

24

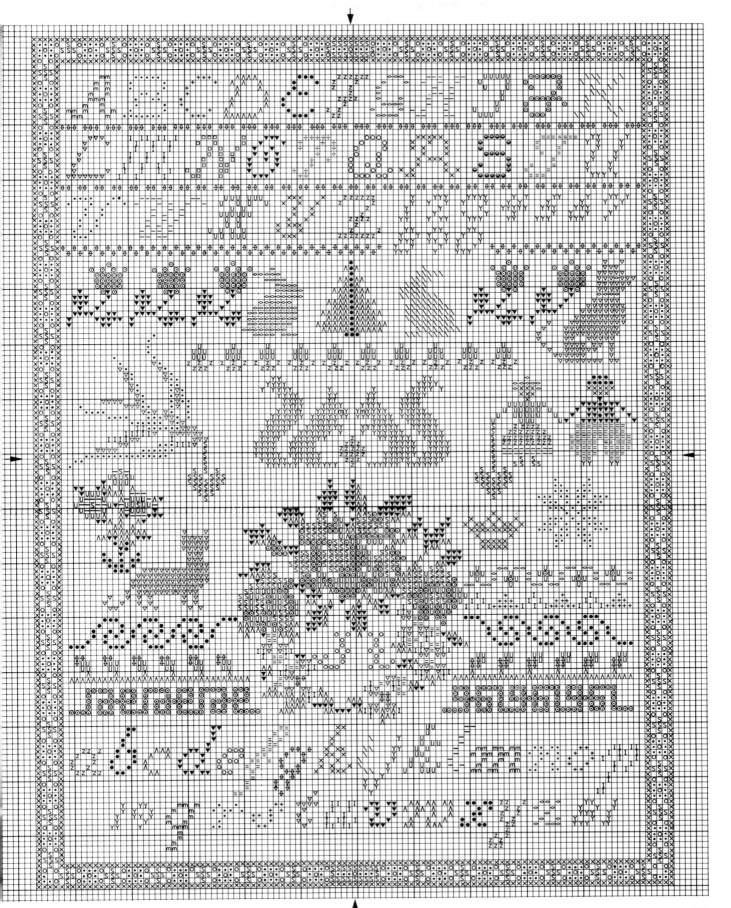

A B C D E F G H I K L M N
O P Q R S T U V W X Y Z.
a b c d e f g h i k l m n o p q r s t u v w x y z.

A B C D E F G H I K L M N O P Q
R S T U V W X Y Z
a b c d e f g h i k l m n o p q r ſ s t u v w x y z.
1 2 3 4 5 6 7 8 9 0

Old English Letter Sampler

In 1890, Elise Schulze embroidered this red-and-white sampler with cotton thread on fine cotton fabric. Such samplers usually were bought stamped and used for needlepoint instruction. The students had to embroider the patterns in close satin stitches and, at the end, select from the embroidered alphabets letters for their names and reproduce them.
Private collection.

This detail of the top illustrated sampler shows the fineness of the satin and stem stitches. The letters of the name embroidered in two colors, were padded with small stitches to provide an embossed effect.

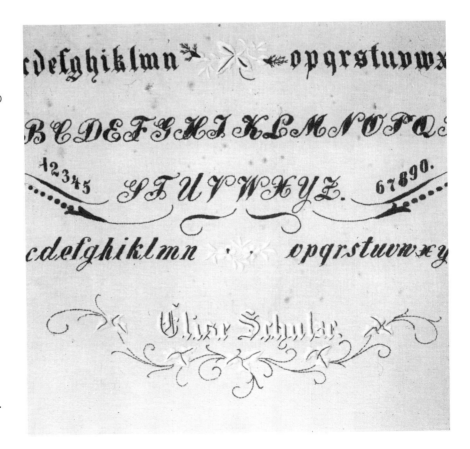

Left
Drawing pattern for the sampler on page 9, bottom, which can be transferred onto the fabric. (See "Transferring Patterns," page 18.)

Shepherd Sampler

The sampler with the shepherd is worked primarily in cross stitch. Only the lower part of the coat, the inner part of the pine tree, as well as the ears of several animals are embroidered in half cross stitch, as the detail on page 29 clearly illustrates. The embroidering is not difficult. But when counting the separate motifs, be very exact if the total impression is to be harmonious. Begin at the top horizontal line; count from the pine tree (2 fabric threads count for one cross). (Counting pattern, pages 30 to 32.) Supplies: 18 colors, cotton embroidery threads corresponding to the color charts on pages 31 and 95; a

canvas needle corresponding in size to the fabric; linen or other evenweave, 24 threads per inch (12 crosses on 1 inch), 20½" × 18½" (50 × 45 cm); white sewing thread.

The finished embroidery is 15" × 13" (38 × 33 cm) including 1¼" hem (3 cm) on all sides. Before beginning the embroidering, baste the center lines with sewing thread. Also overcast the fabric edges with sewing thread to avoid unravelling.

This detail clearly shows how the half cross stitches are worked. At the lower portion of the coat, they run within each line of stitches, beginning at lower left to the upper right, and then from the upper left to the lower right; this produces wavy lines. The ears of the dog are likewise formed from half cross stitches. On the pine tree, the half stitches begin at the crown on the left half of the tree, running on each line from lower left to upper right; on the right side of the tree the stitches run the opposite way, from upper left sloping to lower right.

Counting pattern for the sampler with shepherd and sheep from pages 28 and 29. The left upper portion is found on this page, and on page 31, the right upper part; the remainder of the pattern is on page 32—the left section at the top, and the right section below.

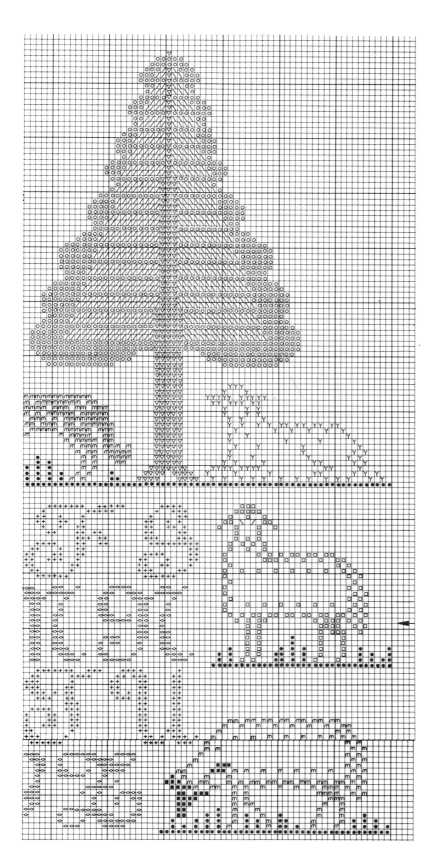

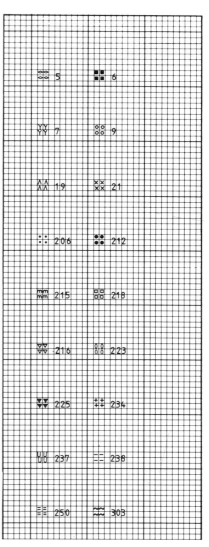

For colors, refer to illustrations on pages 28 to 29 and Color Code Chart, page 95.

Arrows indicate the vertical and horizontal centers of the embroidery.

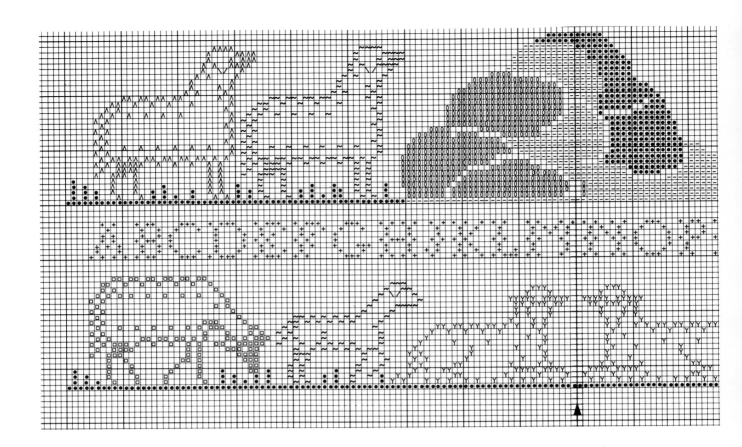

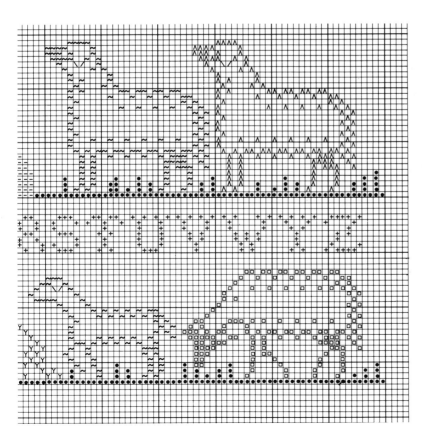

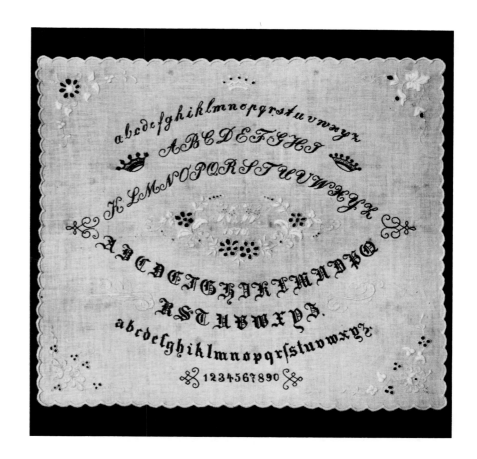

Curved Alphabet Sampler

This fine red-and-white sampler was worked in 1870. In addition to four alphabets, it contains a row of numerals, two crowns and four scroll ornaments in red with white embroidery, embroidered with satin stitch and open work.

To transfer the patterns from pages 34 and 35, use transparent paper to trace both sections of the pattern. Then spread the fabric to be embroidered on a board or working surface, lay transfer paper over the fabric and the transparent paper over it. Secure carefully to avoid slipping and trace pattern using ballpoint pen (see directions, page 18).

Supplies: Cotton fabric needed is the size of the pattern plus 4" (10.2 cm) for the edging and seam folds. If you wish to include the scalloped edge of the original sampler, add 2½" (6.4 cm) on all sides. Embroider with single strand embroidery cotton thread in red and white. *Stitches*: stem stitch, satin stitch, padded satin stitch and buttonhole stitch (page 20). The embroidery can be worked in an embroidery frame.

To finish with scallop edging: use small buttonhole stitches; then cut the fabric inside the contour formed; fold the fabric to the back and overcast the edges with close stitches. When completed, trim the fabric remnants. Small holes can be widened with a piercer such as a knitting needle and then embroidered.

Page 34/35
Drawing pattern for sampler on this page.

abcdefghiklmn

ABCD

KLMNOPQR

N.
187

ABCDEFGH

RSTU

abcdefghiklmn

12345

34

o p q r s t u v w x y z

E F G H I

S T U V W X Y Z

J K L M N O P Q

V W X Y Z.

o p q r s t u v w x y z.

67890

Colored Bead Sampler

An embroidery need not be worked always with colored threads. This example, executed in bead embroidery, features letters, numerals, and motifs. Select embroidery beads in the desired colors, a very fine needle, fine white sewing thread and evenweave fabric, such as *aida* fabric. Evenweave with 14 threads per inch may be substituted, but the *aida* fabric will produce a smoother bead surface.

Follow any counting pattern with each symbol on the pattern corresponding to a bead. Work half crosses, placing the bead on the needle between each stitch out and the new stitch in. The 1976 sampler shown above is only one example; there are no available counting patterns for it. Many embroiderers will prefer to design personal patterns or to revise ideas while embroidering.

Needlepoint Sampler with Flowering Vine

Alphabet in needlepoint technique. This method of embroidering a sampler is unusual; the work has a decorative character. The finished piece is 12½″ × 10¼″ (32 × 25 cm). Embroider half cross stitches in rows working from left to right, beginning at the lower row and working in an upward direction. (See top cross stitch illustration, page 19). *Supplies*: Wool embroidery yarn in eight different colors (for each green background tone, use 3 strands); a canvas needle corresponding to the yarn thickness and 13-count or 14-count canvas, 15″ × 12″ (38 × 31 cm). The finished embroidery should be dampened and stretched on a wooden board until it is completely dry. To finish the edges, fold over and hem in the back. The counting pattern is found on page 38.

For colors, refer to colored illustration of the sampler on page 37.

Two Crowns Red-and-White Sampler

This sampler was embroidered red and white on batiste using fine cotton thread. Stitches: satin stitch, stem stitch, and French knots (pages 20 to 21). The letters, worked in two colors, were embroidered in white satin stitch and then edged with red stem stitch. Some letters were edged in red and the inner surfaces filled in with white French knots.

To create, use washable batiste or fine cotton fabric, red-and-white embroidery cotton thread, single strand; an embroidery needle in corresponding size, and an embroidery frame. Satin stitch (page 20) can most easily be done with an embroidery frame. Instructions for transferring the embroidery pattern onto the fabric are found on page 18.

The pattern drawing for this sampler is on page 40.

0. 6. 8. 2. 9.

6. 7. 8. 9. 0.

1. 2. 3. 4. 5.

1. 2. 3. 4. 5.

Butterfly Sampler

This alphabet and butterfly sampler can be worked from embroidery thread scraps. For this reason, no color chart is given for the pattern drawing on the following two pages. Stem and satin stitches (page 20) are the only necessary stitches. As background, select any fine cotton fabric. Work with an embroidery frame on which the fabric is stretched.

To transfer the pattern drawings from pages 42 and 43 onto the fabric, read "Transferring Patterns," page 18.

Multi-colored A-B-C Sampler

This lovely alphabet sampler was designed and drawn in 1720 by the Augsburg engraver, Martin Engelbrecht. Three letters and an edging detail are illustrated.

Work with cross stitches (see stitch illustration on page 19). This sampler was worked in double size to emphasize the beauty of the letters; the detail of the letter B indicates the interesting color changes.

University of Amsterdam collection.

Cross and Chalice Sampler

Alphabets, borders and religious motifs are highlights of this 1893 sampler from North Germany. Resembling folk art, the stitches are worked in numerous brilliantly colored thick, soft wool yarns on fine evenweave linen. There is no available counting pattern for this sampler.
Engel Textile Museum, Hamburg.

Details of the sampler on page 45 reveal many colors in the flower arrangements chosen for personal preference that are not especially true to nature. The embroidery technique is not predetermined and stitches run in random directions.

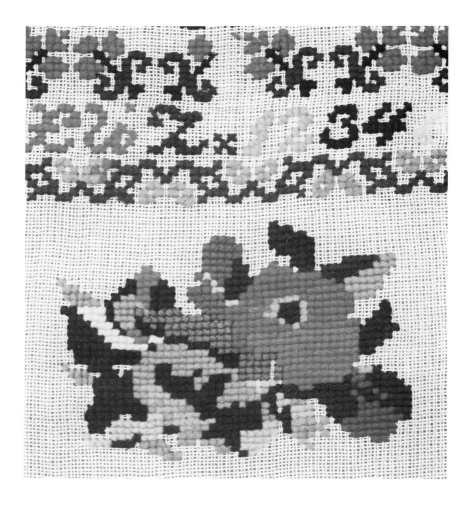

To achieve the shaded effects of the sepals, four colors were used. The tendrils reflect a very individual choice of color, often found in folk art. This heightens the charm of such embroideries.

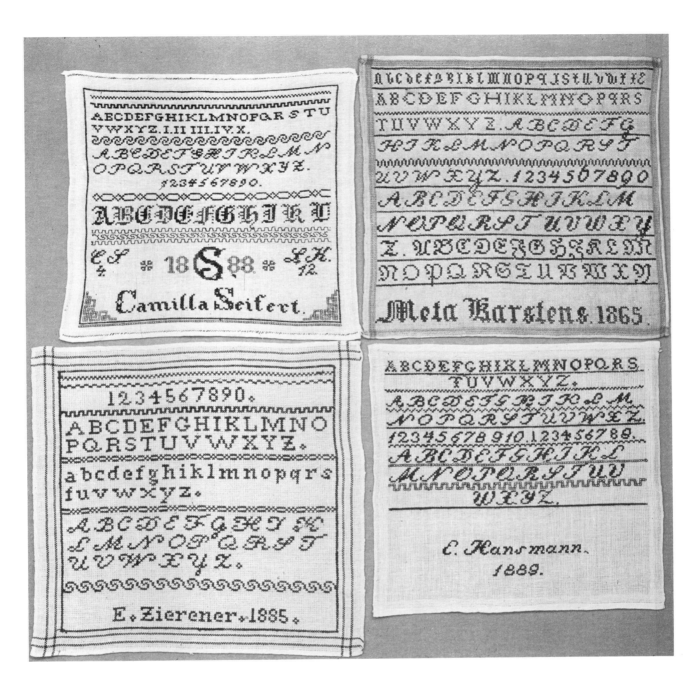

Four Nineteenth Century Samplers

On these four works you can easily observe that the style and arrangement of samplers worked from embroidery instructions between 1865 and 1889 had scarcely changed. Camilla Seifert (upper left) has even included the date,

4. 12. 1888, which you may not notice at first glance. On the Seifert sampler, in addition to cross stitch letters embroidered in two colors, there are also pattern details worked in Holbein (double running) and four-sided stitches. The letters "CS" and "LK" may be the parents' monograms. There is no available counting pattern for this sampler. The count-

ing patterns of the remaining three samplers, worked in red embroidery twist of Danish flower thread in single ply on evenweave, 24 threads per inch, are illustrated on pages 48 to 52. Substitute your own name for the embroiderers', and replace the current year for the original one. These four samplers originated in North Germany.

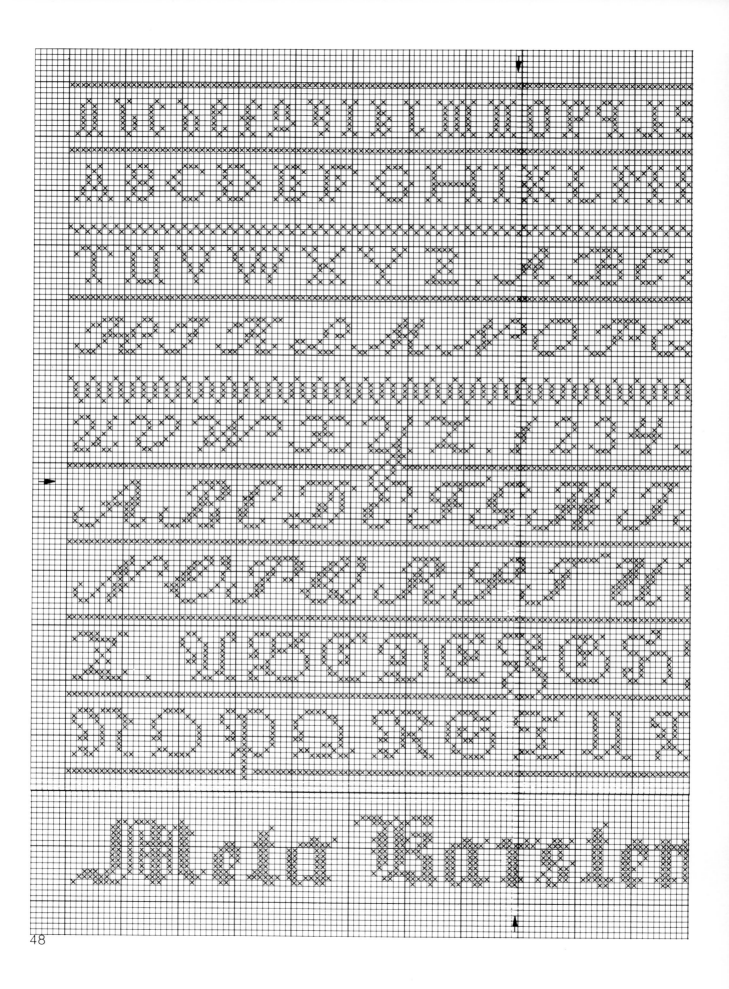

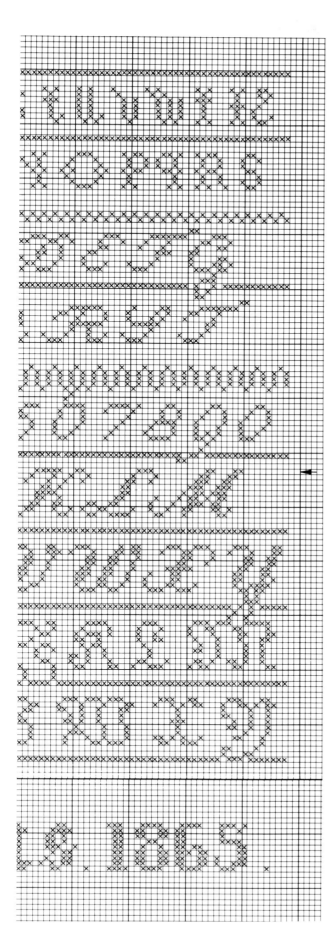

Counting pattern for sampler on page 47, top right. The arrows indicate the vertical and horizontal centers of the embroidery.

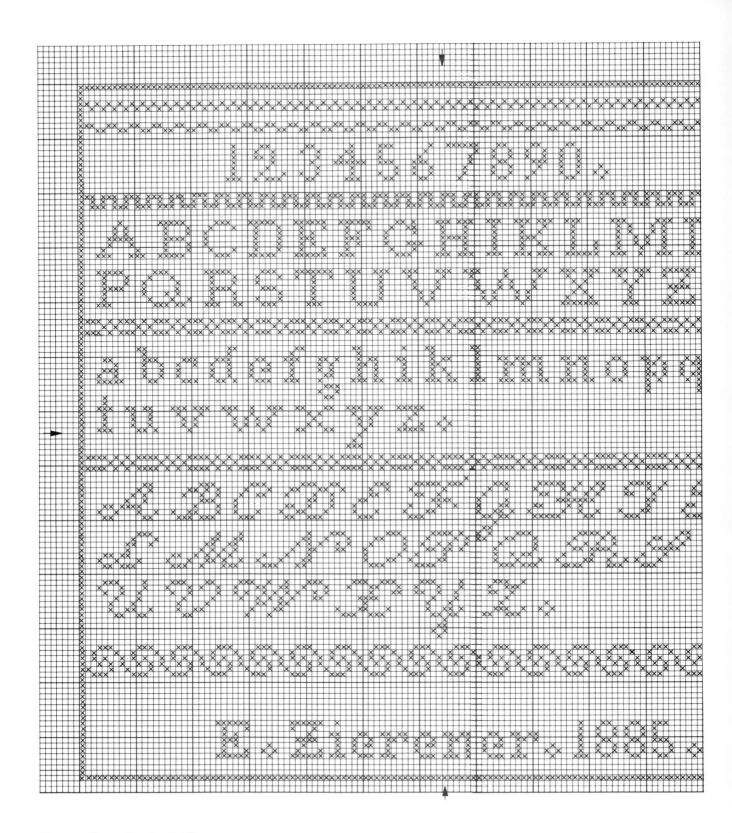

The counting pattern for the E.
Zierener sampler, page 47, lower left;
the right-hand side is illustrated on
page 51. The arrows indicate the vertical and horizontal centers of the
embroidery.

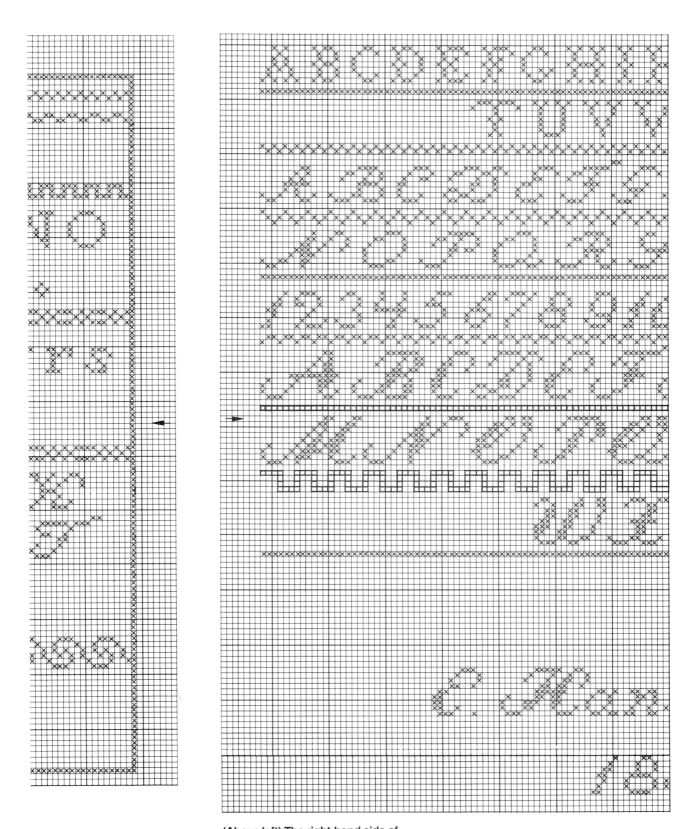

(Above left) The right-hand side of the E. Zierener sampler; (above right) the beginning of the E. Hansmann counting pattern for the sampler, page 47, lower right. (See next page for rest of pattern.)

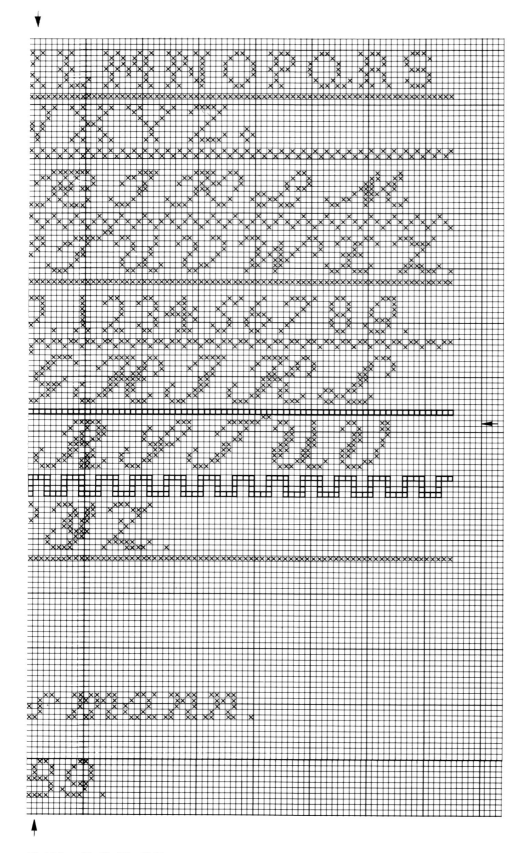

**Right-hand half of the E. Hansmann
counting pattern begun on page 51.
The arrows indicate the vertical and
horizontal centers of the embroidery.**

Swan and Tulip Sampler

Sampler designed from traditional motifs of embroidered curtains, covers and clothing. Size of the embroidery, 15½″ × 16″ (39 × 41 cm). You will need evenweave fabric (24 threads per inch) 18¾″ × 19¾″ (47 × 49 cm) including 1¼″ (3 cm) on all sides for hem.
Threads: Cotton embroidery threads, colors corresponding to symbol script on pages 55 and 95. Canvas needle number 24.

Before beginning the sampler, the fabric edges must be overcast to avoid unravelling. Then baste the vertical and horizontal centers on the evenweave to aid your counting. Begin with the capital "E" of the alphabet; then work towards left and right. This beginning will help you while counting the other letters and motifs. The counting pattern is illustrated on pages 54 to 56.

The counting pattern for the sampler
on page 53. The left half of the upper
part is shown on this page, and the

right half is on page 55. The left
lower part is at the top of page 56;
the right half lower part is below on

page 56. The arrows indicate the vertical and horizontal centers of the
embroidery.

Village Scene, Tree-of-Life and Crowns Sampler

This sampler was inspired by alphabets and motifs from the *Pattern Collections for Old German Linen Embroidery of 1880*[1]. The counting pattern for this sampler is illustrated on pages 58 to 61.

Colors for the single ply embroidery thread are found on pages 60 and 95. *Supplies*: Evenweave linen, 24 threads per inch (12 crosses equal 1 inch), 22″ × 18″ (56 × 46 cm); Danish flower thread or other available embroidery thread; canvas needle appropriate for your evenweave. Size of embroidery, 18″ × 14″ (46 × 36 cm).

Counting pattern for sampler on page 57. Left upper part on this page, right upper part on page 59, left lower part on page 60, and right lower part on page 61. Arrows indicate vertical and horizontal centers of the embroidery.

For colors, refer to color illustration of sampler on page 57 and Color Code Chart, page 95.

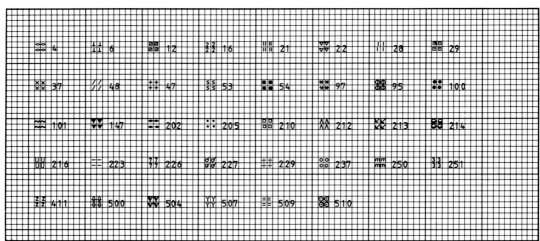

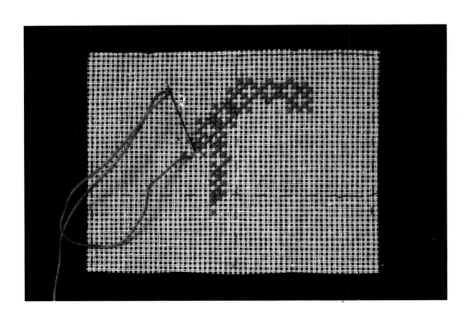

When embroidering on closely woven fabrics, fine canvas must be basted on the embroidery fabric as a guide and later discarded by pulling out the canvas threads separately. This works best if you moisten the fine canvas to loosen before pulling out the threads. Note the needle action through the canvas on the illustration.

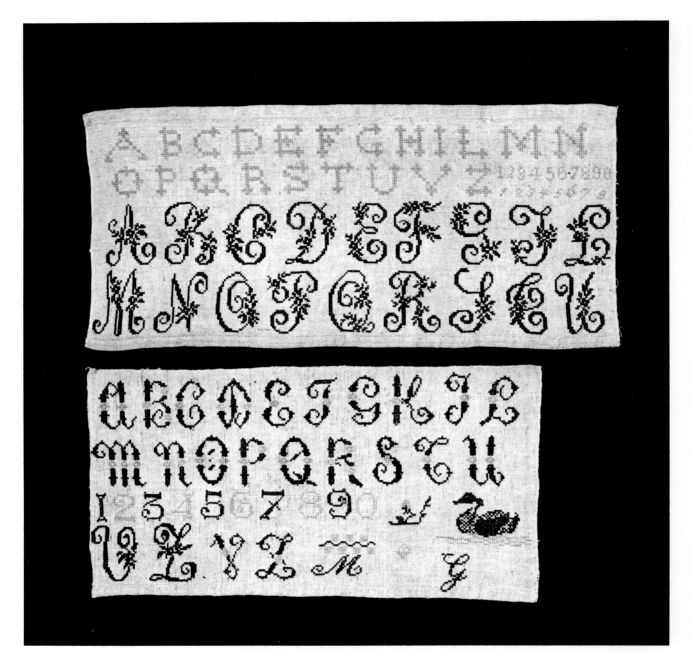

Flowery Samplers

These alphabet samplers present several puzzles: They are embroidered on the same fabrics (grey hand-woven linen), have the same colors (pink, pale blue, dark blue and red), but are, nevertheless, of different sizes. The top one is 21″ × 10″ (53 × 25 cm) and the bottom, 18″ × 10″ (45 × 25 cm). The missing letters "V" and "Z" on the upper sampler are found at the beginning of the last row of the bottom sampler. But letters "V" and "Z" are not missing in other alphabets of both samplers.

The counting patterns for both samplers are found on pages 63 to 67. To embroider, you will need evenweave fabric, 24 threads per inch (12 crosses equal 1 inch), cotton embroidery threads, colors light blue, dark blue and red worked in a single strand thread. For the larger sampler, you will need 24½″ × 13½″ (62 × 34 cm); for the smaller sampler, 21½″ × 13½″ (54 × 34 cm). If you wish, the alphabets of both samplers can be combined in one sampler.

Counting pattern for the upper
sampler on page 62, the left detail.
The center part is illustrated on page
64; the right-hand section on page
65, left. Arrows indicate the vertical
and the horizontal centers of the embroidery.

| | light blue | | dark blue | | red |

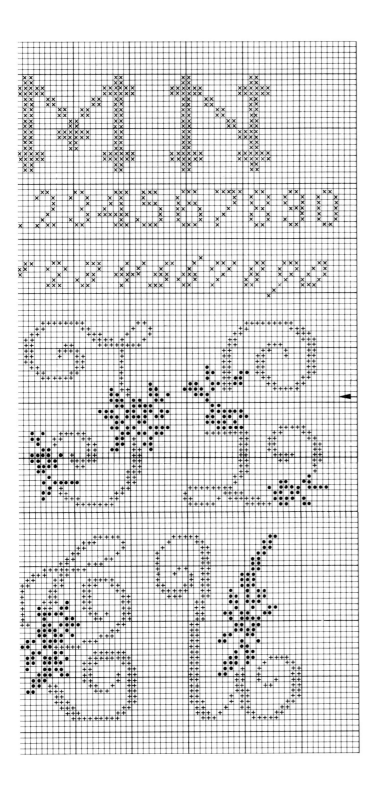

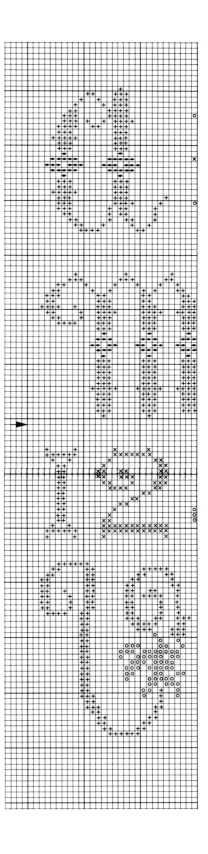

Counting pattern for the upper
sampler on page 62, the right detail.
The left part of the lower sampler,
page 62. Symbols on page 64 indicate the colors (light blue, dark blue
and red) for the embroidery of the
upper sampler.

Counting pattern for the lower
sampler on page 62, the center detail. The right-hand detail of this pattern is shown on page 67; the left on
pages 65 and this page. Arrows indicate the vertical and horizontal centers of the embroidery.

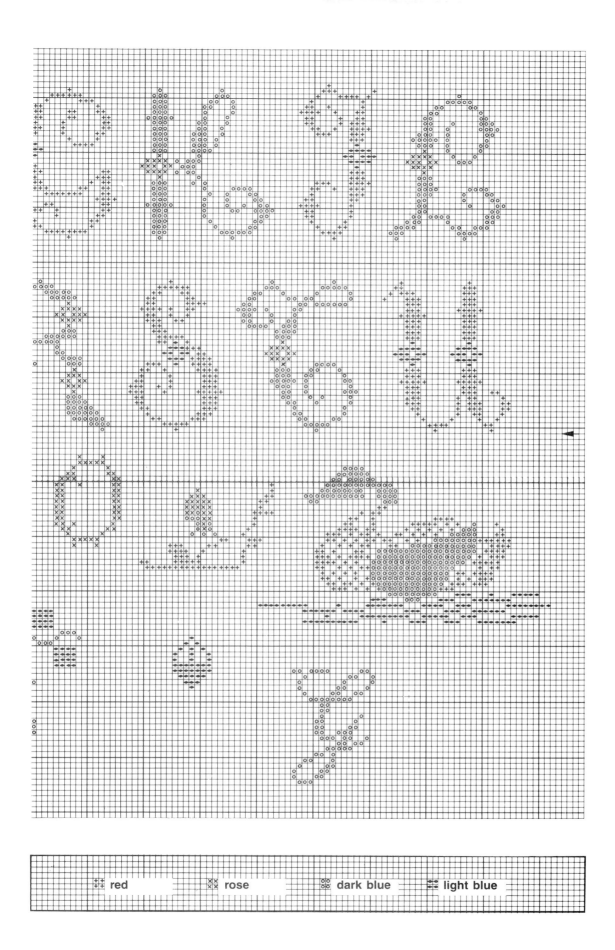

Cherub Sampler

This sampler with cherubs and roses will inspire the creativity of every romantic embroiderer. The motif arrangement and symbolism can be adapted as a commemorative sampler for the birth of a child. For example, instead of the alphabet, embroider the name of the child beneath the rose tendrils, left and right, between the angel groups. Also embroider the initials of the parents and grandparents or godparents. And under the oval (lower center), include the child's birth date; omit the lower row of numerals.

Counting patterns for this embroidery are found on the following three pages. Size of the embroidered area: 16″ × 13″ (40 × 33 cm). *Supplies*: You will need single strand cotton embroidery threads (colors indicated on pages 71 and 95); buy one skein of each color. Even-weave fabric, 24 threads per inch (12 crosses per inch), 19¾″ × 16″ (49 × 40 cm), including hem. Before beginning, overcast the fabric raw edges with sewing thread. Then baste the vertical and horizontal centers onto the evenweave to simplify counting of the fabric threads while embroidering.

Counting pattern for the sampler on page 68 is divided as follows: left upper part, page 69; on this page, right-hand upper detail; the lower left and right portions on page 71. Arrows indicate the vertical and horizontal centers of the embroidery.

70

For colors, refer to color illustration on page 68 and Color Code Chart, page 95.

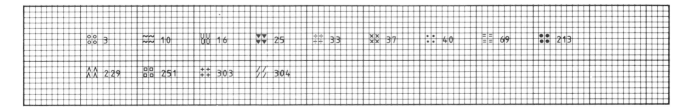

Christiane's Sampler

This multi-colored sampler probably originated around 1890. Presumably, the embroidery results were not exactly the teacher's intention (note the "W" and "P" embroidered over the marked edges). Nevertheless, this sampler is very decorative and quite easy to duplicate.

The counting pattern is illustrated on pages 73 to 75.
Supplies: You will need evenweave fabric, 21 threads per inch (10.5 crosses equal 1 inch), 16" × 14¾" (40 × 37 cm), and allow additional fabric for seams.

Right
Left upper portion of the counting pattern for the sampler shown above.

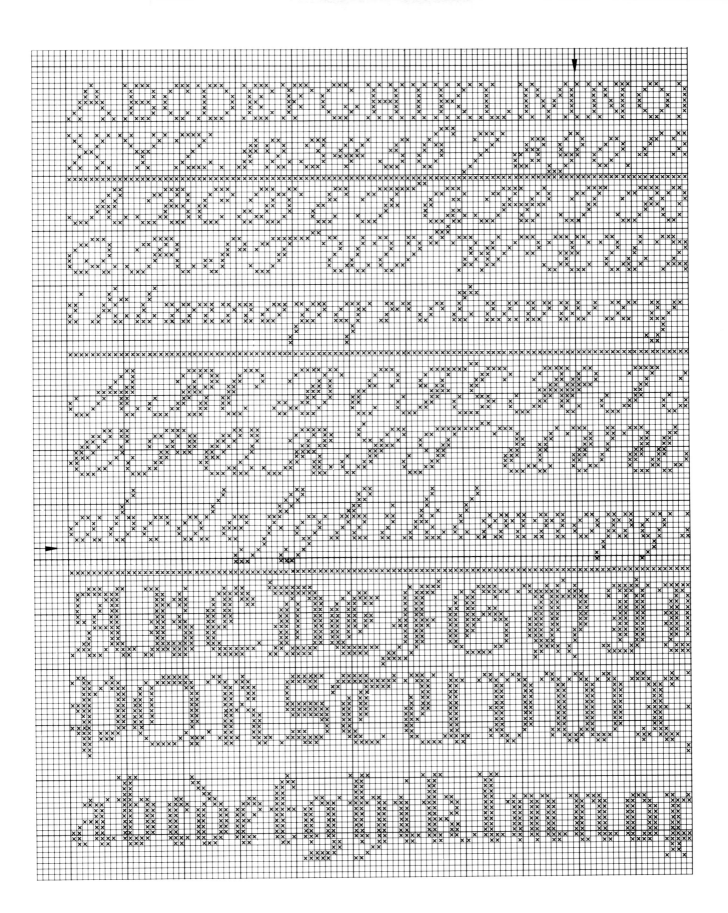

Right upper detail of the sampler on page 72.
Page 75: The remaining lower details of sampler on page 72, left detail above, right detail below.

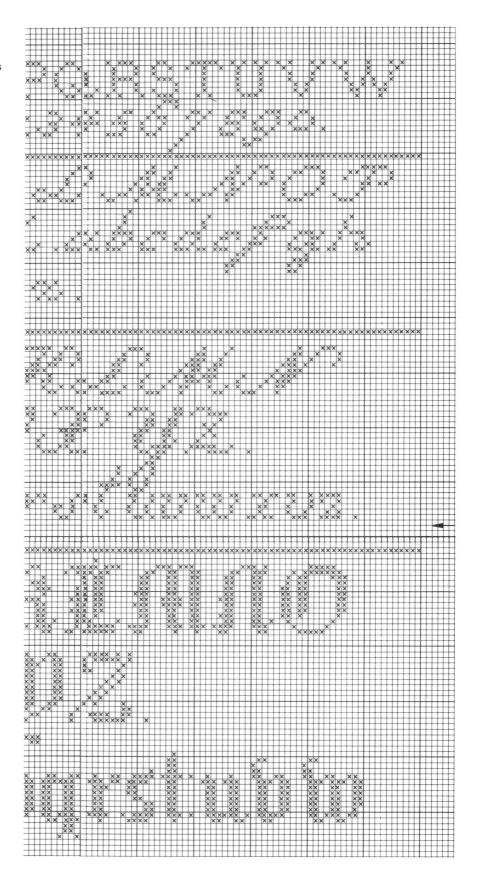

74

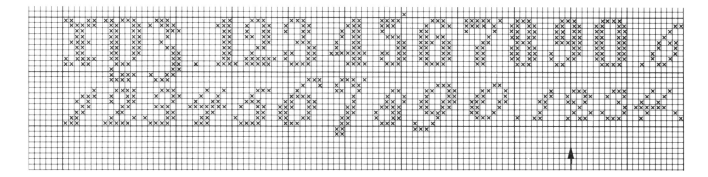

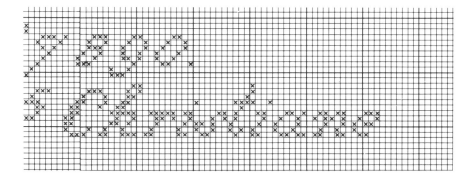

Elizabeth Jane Richards sampler, circa 1800. Red, light and dark blue, gold, pale yellow, cream, white and deep green with light and brown touches on homes and school, tree trunks, windmill and animals. Silk threads on ecru linen, 19¼″ × 13″ (49 × 33 cm). Note the lower center where the motif outlines were transferred directly onto the fabric (and left unworked) while the remainder was completed by covering with the stitches (see page 18 for techniques of transferring).
Victoria and Albert Museum, London.

Bird Border Sampler

A sampler embroidered with one alphabet can also be very attractive. Use single letters for other projects, for instance, as embroidered touches on clothing and other textiles. This composition is based on 22 colors of an old Italian alphabet. The embroidery is 17½″ × 16″ (45 × 41 cm). Counting pattern for this sampler is found on pages 77 to 80. *Supplies:* Cotton embroidery threads, colors corresponding to charts on pages 79 and 95; one skein of each color. Use a canvas needle, number 24. Evenweave fabric, 24 threads per inch (12 crosses equal 1 inch), 21½″ × 20″ (55 × 51 cm); allow 1¼″ (3 cm) on all sides for the hem. To begin the work, overcast the fabric edges with sewing thread to avoid unravelling. Then baste the vertical and horizontal centers with sewing thread to simplify your counting of the fabric threads.

Right
Counting pattern of the above sampler, upper left detail. The arrows indicate the vertical and horizontal centers of the embroidery. Upper right side of the pattern, page 78; lower left, page 79; lower right, page 80.

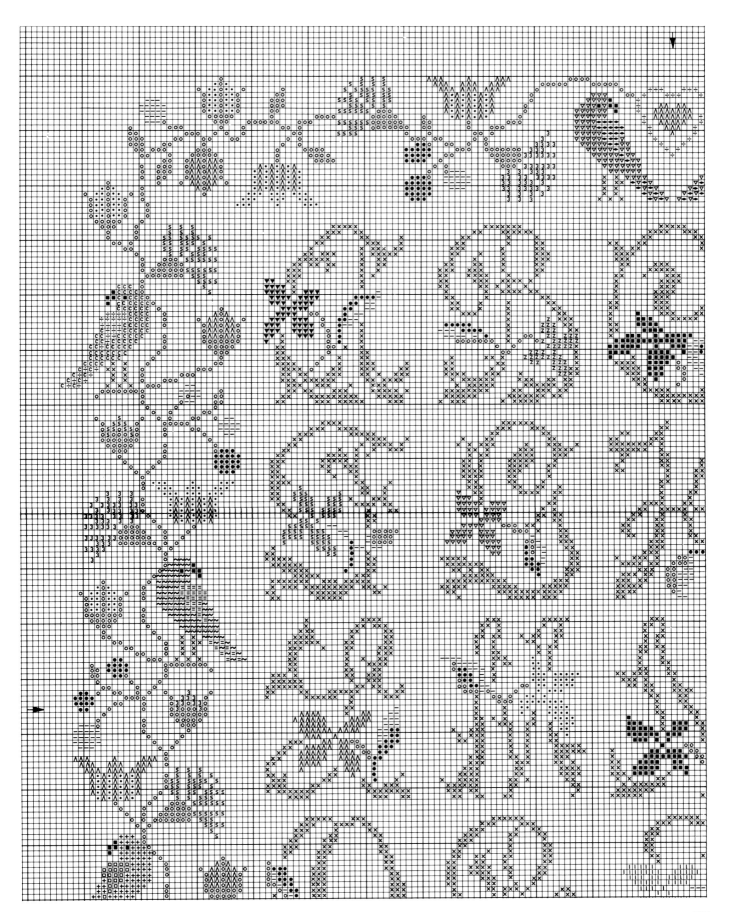

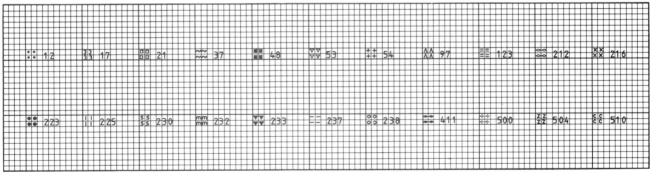

For colors, refer to color illustration
of sampler on page 76 and Color
Code Chart, page 95.

Counting pattern for the sampler on page 76, lower right detail.

Symbolic Motif Sampler

Samplers embroidered with both traditional secular and religious symbols are frequently found on old pieces. These early motifs often have associations and symbolism (begin at upper left):

Easter lamb—Resurrection
Cross, heart and anchor—Belief, love and hope
Tree of life—Renewal
Justice—Righteousness
Well—Well of Jacob; water of life everlasting
Mermaid—Virtue and cleanliness
Lion/Griffin—Strength and bravery
Rooster—Conviction
Mill—Daily bread
Angel with palm—Peace on earth
Sand clock—Change
Key—Key of the Apostle Paul; Key to Heaven
Fruit bowl—Fertility
Dove with heart—Message of love
Dog—Faithfulness and protection
Crown—Royalty; crown of Jesus; crown of life; belief

Counting patterns are found on pages 82 to 84.
Supplies: You will need *aida* fabric or comparable evenweave, 14 threads per inch (7 crosses equal 1 inch); Swedish linen thread or substitute cotton embroidery thread; colors corresponding to above illustration; canvas needle suitable for your thread.

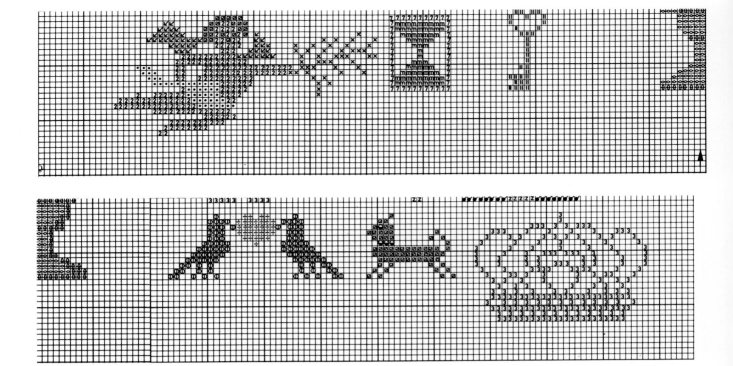

The counting pattern for the sampler on page 81 was divided as follows: Left upper part, page 82; right upper part, page 83; on this page: Left lower part (top); right lower part (middle). Arrows indicate the vertical and horizontal centers of the embroidery. For colors, refer to color illustration of sampler on page 81.

Adam and Eve and Tree of Life Sampler

The sampler at the right (page 85) may be re-created; or the motifs may be used in your own sampler creations. Finished size: 24″ × 16¼″ (61 × 41 cm). Supplies: You will need evenweave, 24 threads per inch (12 crosses equal 1 inch), 30″ × 20″ (75 × 50 cm), which includes hem allowance; cotton embroidery threads; colors corresponding to illustration; canvas needle, number 24. Counting patterns for the sampler and blank frame (at top) are available on pages 86 to 90.

**Adam and Eve and Tree of Life
Sampler**

Counting pattern for the sampler on
page 85, left upper part; center left
detail, page 88. Arrows indicating the
horizontal centers are found on
pages 88 to 89.

Counting pattern for the sampler on
page 85, right upper part; middle
section, page 89. Arrows indicate the
horizontal center of the sampler.

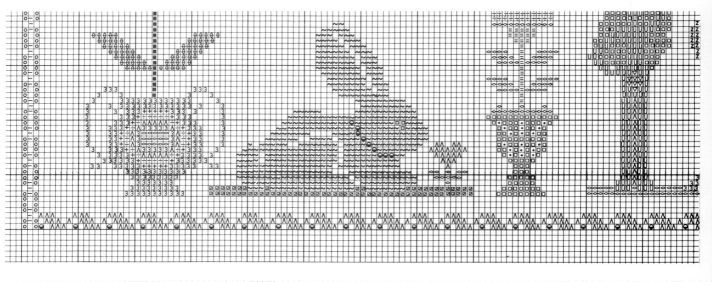

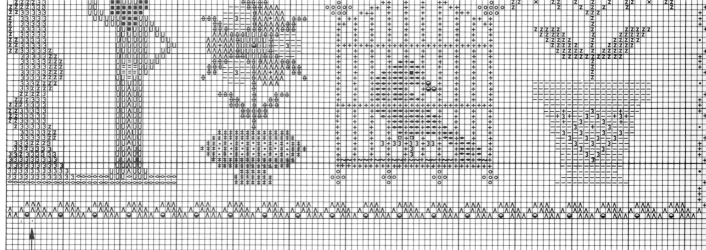

Above
Counting pattern (lower details) for
the sampler on page 85. Please refer
to color illustration, page 85, for your
color choices.

Right: A detail of the blank frame on
the upper edge of the sampler, page
85, indicating how to embroider the
corner and border.

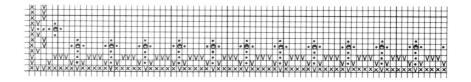

"The Ways of the Lord Are Right" Sampler

The Ways Of The Lord Are Right, embroidered by Linda Brown, re-creates samplers her mother and grandmother had embroidered in their younger years. Linda's grandmother had embroidered hers with silk on linsey-woolsey; her mother with cotton on linen; Linda worked this sampler with wool on canvas. Flowerpots are embroidered in vertical satin stitches; all others are cross stitches. Counting patterns for this sampler are found to the right and on the following page. *Supplies*: Double canvas, 21" × 17" (53.3 × 43.2 cm), wool yarn of your own favorite color choices; canvas needle suitable for the yarn and canvas.

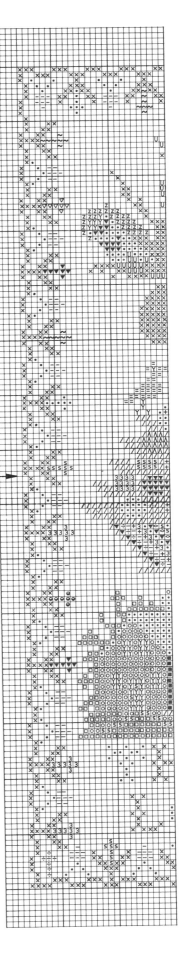

Lovebirds Sampler

A project for impatient creators: This sampler is quickly reproduced on *aida* fabric or other evenweave with comparable threads per inch. The finished piece is 18″ × 13″ (45.7 × 33.5 cm). *Supplies*: You will need *aida* fabric, 14 threads per inch, 22″ × 17″ (55.9 × 43.2 cm) which includes hem allowance on all sides; linen thread (or other suitable thread) corresponding to colors of illustration; 2 skeins each of leaf green, beige and chestnut, one skein of each other color; canvas needle. When embroidering with linen thread, it will "pill" and lose its smoothness. To avoid roughness, work with short threads and continue twisting the thread as you embroider. Before beginning the embroidery, overcast the edges of the *aida* fabric to avoid unravelling. Baste the vertical and horizontal centers on the fabric, using sewing thread, to help guide you as you count (these markings will be removed after completing the embroidery).

Counting patterns for the above sampler, below (upper detail) and on the following page.

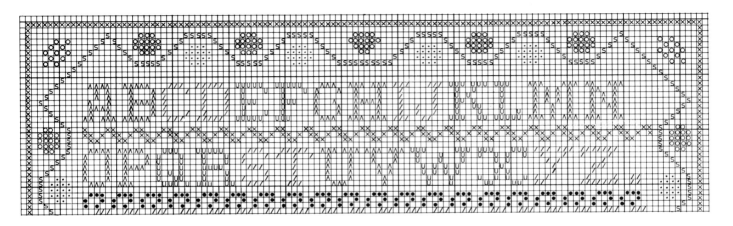

For colors, refer to color illustration on page 93.

Appendix

Color Code Chart

Numbers refer to Danish flower thread colors which are identified as closely as possible by name. You may substitute other available threads. Select colors for your embroidery that are harmonious and also pleasing to you.*

0	white	29	deep raspberry-brown	215	dark linen
2	medium pink (rosy)	31	medium canary yellow	216	medium peat brown (greyish)
3	medium pink (greyish)	32	medium grey	217	dark blue-green
4	medium reddish brown	33	clear sky blue	218	greenish cream
5	dark violet (dull)	34	medium yellow-green	220	light navy blue
6	pale greenish gold	35	light grey (bluish)	222	medium linen
7	pale grey-beige	37	medium magenta	223	medium yellow-green (greyish)
8	light laurel green	40	medium almond green	224	medium grey-green
9	dark laurel green (greyish)	47	medium yellow-gold	225	creamy yellow
10	medium grey-green	48	bright orange-gold	226	medium blue-green (greyish)
11	medium mauve	51	yellow	227	medium blue-grey
12	very pale apricot (greyish)	53	light tangerine	228	dark blue-grey
13	deep rosy beige	54	medium gold (orangey)	229	medium cloudy sky blue
14	deep rosy rust	69	medium rose pink	230	medium periwinkle blue
15	medium terra cotta	86	pinky-orange	231	pale grey (greenish)
16	rich creamy yellow	88	medium raspberry	232	pale pink-violet
17	medium bright cobalt blue	92	cranberry red	233	medium lilac
19	light grey	93	pale orange	234	deep violet (greyish)
21	medium greyish blue	95	dark coral	235	pinky grey
22	medium sky blue	96	rosy caramel	236	light gold (greenish)
23	deep blue-violet	97	cardinal red	237	medium olive green
25	whitish beige	99	pale apple green	238	deep grass green
26	medium greenish gold	100	medium grass green	242	light blue-green
28	pale cream	101	light grass green	250	light terra cotta
		113	medium geranium	251	light peat brown (greyish)
		123	bright canary yellow	260	light yellow-green
		130	medium cobalt blue	280	dark yellow-green
		131	light cobalt blue	302	pale grey-green
		147	black	303	very pale grey
		148	bright cobalt blue	304	pale blue (greyish)
		201	blue-black	441	dark peat brown
		202	dark navy blue	500	deep geranium
		203	rich gold	503	rosy apricot
		205	rich rose-violet	504	orange
		206	deep moss green (greyish)	505	bright yellow-green
		210	dark turquoise (greyish)	506	medium yellow-green
		211	medium turquoise	507	bright spring green
		212	medium moss green	508	deep apple green
		213	deep caramel	509	bright jade
		214	rich chestnut	510	bright azure blue

Notes

HISTORICAL DEVELOPMENT

1. *Schönspergers Modelbuch von 1597.*
2. *Leitfaden für den Unterricht in den weiblichen Handarbeiten.*
3. *Der Handarbeitsunterricht als Klassen-Unterricht.*
4. *Furm-oder Modelbüchlein.*
5. *Ein new Modelbuch.*
6. *Eyn newe kunstlich moedtelbuch alle kunstner: zo brauchen fur snyrzeller/wapensticker/ perlensticker, etc.*
7. *Schön newes Modelbuch.*
8. *Zeichen-, Maler- und Stickerbuch zur Selbstbelehrung für Damen.*

DESIGNS and PROJECTS

1. *Mustersammlung für altdeutsche Leinenstickerei 1880.*

*Sterling Publishing Co., Inc. appreciates the cooperation of Ginnie Thompson Originals (Box 930, Pawleys Island, SC 29585) and the Counted Thread Society of America (3305 S. Newport St., Denver, CO 80224)

Index